1962

This book may be kept

The Night of the Hammer

THE NIGHT OF THE HAMMER

Poems by Ned O'Gorman

Harcourt, Brace and Company HB *New York*

Contents

811.5
O35

To Annette de Bouthillier-Chavigny O'Gorman

A POEM ABOUT A PRINCE

The boy came cooped in gold to France
between a copper drum
and batteries of tuscan birds.
When he appeared among the halls
they swaddled him in satin shirts
rolled him marbles on
an ivory floor.
Countesses with paper skin
brought him purities of fish
the Indian minnow, the chinese
whale. A marquis with velvet hair
brought him pails of rabbit eyes
and images in stone and leaf.
A cardinal seismic with a golden
stammer a grizzle hound and livid
equatorial tree.
         And he sat
and dreamed while turks grew white
and cavemen danced the saraband
and captains in a northern sea
scraped doubloons loose
from Triton's eyes.
         Once when
he had played his part
and sat alone, impenetrable,
he brought his chamois hand across
the rivers of a golden harp
            and
Lo the darkness moved a bit
for within that lovely doric head
music ran askelter up
and touched its finger on his crown
and there was nothing else to do
but play and write the whole thing down.

CHILDHOOD

Childhood is when the mouth tastes earth.
When the body is the body's sign;
When there is no studied end to time;
When hands join and make a cradle.

The child races through the snow in circles
and hears on the swing the sound of air;
the world's grave mummery is everywhere
and the sun like a falcon swerves toward his wrist.

There are drummers drumming and red sails
making April conquests in the bay;
the flesh is still a flurried sound of clay;
kites go as high as God and there are birds.

Though children are not passionate
they feel the thigh against the sheet;
When there is thunder they will weep;
Stairs go down to halls and rooms are darknesses.

The child is verb and hieroglyphic of his day
and sits and broods like a thinking flame;
That is called the playing of the game;
A child tends to glory like a pirate in a church.

And suffering fills him up with light
that holds its lumen for another time;
And one day as he plays he'll see a sign
and lift his arms and cry aloud like Man.

TO MY FATHER

O thou sweet dumb-bell
deceiver of my christmases,
plaything, tricker of tricksters,
genitor, speller, grace of the kitchen,
feller of trees, gallant, delineator,
simpleton, follower of girls,
renown of manner, dominus and calamitatum,
I come to you careless and bright from games
with thy paternity.

O thou beauty, brightness,
bearer of horses and flaring pennants,
I've followed you among
dark terraces and lawns, where dragged
in speculation I read you out
and busy with gesture and kiss I sang
of filial increase. I come to you
clamoring and quick, your oracle
and fragment.

O fisher, pillager,
I ask that you receive me
after years of silence among
the wars of parents and their love
fraught with stratagem, where boyhood dark
as a cove bruited with light. Study me
with tape and rule, fix yourself along
this alphabet and learn, my father,
my face.

THE RESURRECTION OF ANIMALS

I had a dream and heard animals
called wanderers who had no use
except as food or play, but
went to pieces in the flourish
of animal sleep, caught
by the knives and fires
so long hungry in their blood.

Whoever said that had no eye for glory.
But must have been a butcher or
a lonely man who had found life
full of killing and full of expectation.

Who has not animal has no good thing
in his blood but manhood gone wild
with manhood or lady gone wild with mirror.
Not tricked with the lovely passion of a mind
man fears the animal who sees the animal
he's hid so well. It crosses the bridges
of his wilderness and corners him
in the wood where
the fox calls brother and the eagle
reels without caution near his eyes.

There will be animals in heaven
bright as we though as they were
since they did not think of God.
But they will change to what they were again
and face the hunter in their master's eyes.

THE AUNT

When children are very young
aunts can be quite anyone
who is old and unremarkable.
This aunt was archetypically correct,

doubting children and their dogs,
aching when it rained, praying for accord
between the sexes and the late arrival.
Content with nothing if it were right. . . .

When I was young I thought of God
as color and found that it was hard
to banish him to blue or white,
the colors I knew from watching.

Once when I was ill and wrapped in bed,
at five o'clock my Aunt stood at my head
and swished me with her crinkled hand.
And, as she bent to kiss me, I saw descending

an assault of color, moving in the air,
a troop of peacocks' tails, a flair
of spectrum wrenched from light.
Astounded with this sudden firework

I carefully constructed God again,
his temper and his mind, his ken,
his fatal hand, and discovered
my Aunt had carried on her head

My God without a single angel
to help her with the load.
                        When will
the Aunt reveal again the answer and
the question: Quem colorem habet Sapientia?

SING MY MOUTH

Sing my mouth of animal eyes,
of gold and taste of gold close knitted,
sing my mouth of human goods
of gold and gold sweet tasted.

Let fires turn the tiger's bleat
toward the marauding army,
and turn the violence of the sword
into the timbrel of the dove.

Against the eye the bone is pitted
jarring rubies from the hand,
breaking the snarling of the ape
into the croaking of the lamb.

In the branched silence of a tree
a nightingale will tremble high.
Beneath, an alligator burns
As thirty thousand eagles sigh.

VIEWS OF A VALLEY (*Lo Speco, Narni*)

I *Roosters*

They sound as if they had no sense
and razed their body every time they croaked.
But they recall to me the way of fowl
more than gabbles of duck or arrays of pheasant do:
being so many quandaries of birds in a simian bush
hid with trouble in the rooster's throat.

II *Clouds*

Being close to clouds is
conflicting. Straight ahead
and on the level of your eyes
they move or not, but touched
by the wind's intelligence
they back up on each other
inconsequential as sticks.

Being so close I tend to see
clouds from another point
of view—as glories, at least
what we tend to think
glories are—
the intellect's loud glory,
all the middling excellence
of cats, the positive demeanor
of my father, trees, fire
in the garden—these glories
(precious things) seen from
this high Umbrian gallery
break precious near to nothing
because conflicting with heaven
clouds, like glories,
tend to fascination and paralysis.

CUCKOOS

A song like that I'd sing to a fox.
Though I'm no follower of the chase
I fear the slaughter
in all bestial things.

Let this be said of the cuckoo's song:
within the shafts of animals
I hear the slaughter
of the dinosaur's whoop;

But the cuckoo's song is honed,
straitened and nothing nuptial:
the intellect's bark,
the simpleton's jog.

No sound like that comes from a beak.
I heard it once at night
and held the door
against antipodes.

EASTER AMONG FOUR CHILDREN

(FOR GIULIA AND GEORGE)

When blessed lord had opened up the cave
to flee with celebration into god
he left the noise of children in the hall
to keep some bellowing on the edge of sense.

I know four loudly shouting children
who bring increase of sound to sound
and tip tin cups of water to the ground
like prophets breaking laws upon the sand.

Grae, the brooding sport, breathless from
a chase among the lilacs, discovers in a
pandemonium of bells the hidden mille miglia
in the day (thus gulls awake the fox).

Anna, wound in the flag of Greece, comes out
the wall like Helen fresh from buzzing Paris
out of bed, swinging her cap as though
she wore a silver buckle from his boot.

Dino, bedded down in wool, does battle with
his machina of nerves and from a trinity of chin
spits out the orange rind and stays amid
his rash the grandeur of the eight-month child.

Tina, brim with disaster, sits and reads
how much the dragon loved the maid
and when the knife drives in she rises up
in ponderation of Saint George and smiles.

And three, the poet, the philadelphian and his
lady sit among the conquest of the tribe
and watch how blessed lord walked out the tomb
to race with all his angels through the April wheat.

THE SWING

Once in the air I'll not come down
until my eyes are cleared of
sound and filled with sights
I have not touched and stones I
have not found. Enemies
cannot reveal the food of love
nor lovers how the kiss should be
but in the air I'll play
battue with lights, receive
the serpent with my foot
and understand for all I've
learned why Thales died
(if all were water) why trees
burn down (if all is flame)
and why when stars shine in my
room I hear the theory of pain.
I shall swing, swing beyond
myself to rock with every hurt
of wind and slumber in the coming
down in speed of light and graphs of stone.

A SONG FOR THE PASSIONATE

I tell you stop, be human, feel the cheek
flat upon the pillow, the arms resting
sole across the breast. Learn the night.
Hands can lie and not touch, can rest
and not bear weight. The belly is without
passion in an empty bed. Alone to itself
a face can enter in the head and lurk there
and become a loved one without a bonnet.
It is not very hostile to know that neck
and spine are not necessarily touched
by lips into life; not Eden nor spring
need the visit of children (though children
are gracious and bear watching) the body
needs the neither-here-nor-there of God,
the sluggard vein, that you my indolent
girl burn to the very hottest resurrection.

A DESCRIPTION OF THE SEA
FOR LINA LENZI
WHO HAS NEVER SEEN IT

There is no reason in it.
It is known by extravagance.
Think how the water falls
over the hill when you tip
a copper dish after washing.
The descent is torrential
like unfolding a sheet
in the sun. A residential
sea made from the tasks
of a Tuscan day. That's
the sea, a morning's wifery.

There's a green light in it.
Think of the branches
of those umbrella pines
that catch green beneath them
as a cardinal crowds
all scarlet on his head.
Or a salamander lost
in thoughts of furnaces and flints
waits among the honeysuckle
where bees, hammers in their wings,
build pontoons across seas of lights.

There's the noise of the noon
bus in it, like a swoon
of girls hollering with rage
that Tom, decrepit cat, had
chewed their darling captive
in its cage. Or a fix of soldiers
pale from urging priests from sleep
and saints from pinnacles
rail on a hill and rock the air
with cannon. That's the sea,
my simile of the mind's famine.

There's the black of night in it.
Watch the valley from Vespucci's
tower when the Arno cracks the ark
of heaven and the pines pull
together like a line of quail
who sight the barrel through
the bush. The moon turns
the furrows of the sea
and alters then the scape and
the span of it, in imitation
of these black and natural things.

The sun glares through light
like a girl following a wasp
down her first communion veil;
or oxen touching fire with
their red pompons. It's the rain
of every spring since partisans
lost among the poppies closed
their eyes to dream the Tiber
from their tears. In the building
of an April night the world
contrives its salts and ambergris.

The sea's the world's hot fiber,
the caterwauling cosmology
of the brainless love of God.
The sea is the lexicon of
gardens and the weight of winds.
It has no sweetness of streams
nor has it any bottomside like
pools. The sea's a net of water,
a prairie of sunken barge and
sides of mountains only climbed
by fish. I tell you, travel to it!

I AM A DULL MOSAIC BOY

I am a dull mosaic boy
byzantine and fluid-eyed,
fey, collapsed with falling down
the passages along the sun.

Wide-eyed and crazed, procession wise,
accustomed to the length of days
when princes stood along the wall
astounded and amazed.

Numb and dazzled, drenched in gold
from head to toe I'm struck,
becoming slowly like a rose
in tesserae of gold bedazed.

This dark comparison I hold
above me, high and still,
stuns music into ambergris,
myself to accomplished loveliness.

And in this, the very start of youth,
remarkable seems the day,
for I am dull, mosaic, masked,
with head of rose, in thunder cast.

THE TUNNEL

Raloo, raloo this apple root
shadow of a bitter core,
black and deep (raloo) it is
this hundred colored fruit.

Tin soldier in a navy boat
trundles down the base of it
(raloo) where I espy the tents
of bats and nests of ghosts.

It lies in winter covered
still (raloo) when apples
clamber in the branch
all pulse and undiscovered.

Raloo, raloo this tunnel tree
where the apple fruit will grow
is canopy and entrance to
the hideout of my soul (ralee).

A LOVE SONG TO BE SUNG WITHOUT MEASURE

I set my mind upon the names of love
and dreamed I slept in the sun's music
and knelt beside your body, beautiful
as birds flying, separate as Shem,
deliberate as a cage.

The grace your body is sloped into the ground
and I set apples and brass bowls upon a stream,
heard a wind, saw a light; balance left my face,
sirens shook the trees and I gathered darkness
like a hood, drew myself into a line and fled
among the weeds.

Your sleep's the sleep of those who made for
adoration cannot adore. The trapeze of your walk
sum of shadow, subtraction of light; your self
burning in my mind, flings like a windlass and
spires in an Indian crown about my head.

The wish of thunder in the rose
the garden in the monolithic sky
Elijah caught in the owl's hoot
God hid in the heron
the peacock's tonnage of plume
break from your sleep in the chamber
where I alone keep vigil in this illusion.

You will rise up, pick your scarf from
the branch, walk away no darker with my dream,
not dizzy with all the lamentation I sowed
your sleeping eyes. For the law of love
written everywhere broods above you with its
cormorant head and body shaped in the shape of flame.

AN OCCURRENCE IN AN ACRE

I saw it there at the joining
of two streams. Two streams
and a rock at the joining.
An occurrence in an acre—
nothing to wonder at,
this wall that simplified and straightened.

Water flashed at my feet,
my hand reached for the rock,
toward the marriages of suns
and the beginning. I held it
in the light, the world's weight
and petrification; polyhedron which dazzled.

A hand shifted calipers within
the earth. There was a great hush
in my arm. I held the closet of emeralds;
sea horses galloped to coral.
I fell in the tilt of the sea.
O copy-book of elves; I'd touched entelechy.

A DYNASTIC POEM

When first I learned it was no clatter
in our corded blood that made that
stammer in your brain, I thought our
fragile tribe would break like herons
in a winter wind. This name knew
sorrows in its first lurch from ape;
seasons had no more sound of going
than our tribe; no child ever knew
the rules of hazard games as we knew
interlude of viper and the thorny hoop.
We'd lost all elegance and wit;
the widow's joy that lets her loose
her veil and go with all her kin
to find the stud in Orion's belt;
the excursion of the ruined girl
who threads another ribbon in her blouse.
O guard your walk. Go tenderly and run
the hills in attention; leap not too high
nor snare the quickest beast that runs.
Sleep. Do no aerial act; learn the day.
We watch, each in Darien or Rome,
not the intrusion in your skull but
your high exercise of will that gives
us thought of two who fixed the verb
and glory of our blood: the red-haired
boy who hanging from a chandelier
in Cork called all the state to bless
him libertine and that lustbucket prince
who pulled brambles from the ground of France
and made sapped priests to new again.

ONE MORNING

My lover comes down.
His lion sold for nothing.
No growl, no skirmish.
My lover comes down
And I am fortunate.

My lover comes down.
The chimney hammers
At the hearth. O!
Feasting means nothing.
My lover comes down.

Let him talk to stones.
Eat at noonday. Walk alone.
He will perform a task.
He will perform a task.
Be disinterested in everything.

My bought lover comes down.
Find the lace napkin.
Unhitch the stallion. Field him.
Set the grill before the fire.

My lover, my pauper,
Comes down where I sleep.
The cut worm cuts the scythe.
Tangles with me.
My lover comes down.

He will walk where he cannot.
He will pretend. Greet him.
When he leaves, mark his body,
Insignia and amazing shell.
He will leave you as you are. Dark.

THE KISS

Talk of passion is a winter thing,
a huddle of girls, descending wind.
There is no vehicle in a kiss
to carry fury and originality.
In that wherewithal of mouth
the body greets with cannon
the profundis and halt clamavi
of the virgin. Dying is a kiss,
it has broken me. It rimes with tiger
and the gallow tree.

A CONSIDERATION OF HIS LADY

She was divine, I told it to her face.
Not easy to be a deity:
divinities have crimped their hair
and walk upright on two feet.
Footsore these divinities. I'd make her
topnotch, the reverted witch,
faulty on her feet.

"O I've no chance of beauty any more."
And held her mirror to her dying face.
She cried she'd die a pauper
with no pennies on her eyes.
The light would not completely stop
but enter in and scorch
the coffin lid.

There was nothing I could do.
No ceremony would break her down;
no garlic to push between her teeth.
She was divine, I told it to her face—
but she was woman and could not
bear distractions
and the thought of time.

I let her sit there like a Tuscan
tomb, propped on her elbow
in the dark. I could not think
but heard her sorrowing. Yet in her mind
she dreamed a staff of bells,
this crazy saint
sleeping out her dark night.

THE FOX

In a dominant wood the fox
is emerald among the branches,
being all eye in a natural night,
all mortal in a book!

There cannot be a book about a fox,
toying with the playful snake,
watching the face on the starling's wing,
enumerating.

The fox is all jape and leap,
scream, collision, scud, pavane,
wide-leaping, Iago in a snare,
all tumult the fox is.

The inclination of the planetary sense,
an Ethiope image, collapsing, gives us the fox,
anti-functional, but
delicately, utterly, fox.

A SONG FOR EILEEN'S MARRIAGE

Some are made for marriages
and build the artifact of love.
Some are walled in silences
to know the darknesses of love.

One there is who'll marry
when summer and its sun are high.
Who'll walk with whispering ear-ringed girls
to marriage with an ebon boy.

His manhood is a certain dark
a dignity and gist of flame,
and ladyhood will hover there
and speak a sweet Florentian name.

When bridegroom shudders like a hand
and the sun of summer sings
race will make exchange of grief
and lose itself in marriaging.

Then wedding like a quiet tree
will make a balance in the night
when alabaster windows break
and fall in iliads of light.

A DIRGE

It shall be called your animal sorrow
with platonic brow, battered to jewel
when God stooped to laugh.
                    Either Jeremy
of man or Ruth of woman is burned
in your face resting like an arc
an Indian girl wears for beauty.

His memory is young with morning,
vagrant boy with the marvelous limbs,
girl whose body holds a tree
bends your funeral in the night
to pitch so dark you cannot see.

But there is a bit of death
in the making of the race.

Half the world was made when God made the dead.

THE ROSE AND THE BODY OF THE ROSE

The rose and the body of the rose
the stem, the balustrade of air
the pith of darkness in the fist
the rose and the body of the rose.

The wolf and the body of the wolf
the jaw and the marrow in the skull
the furnace fastened in the eye
the wolf and the body of the wolf.

The wren and the body of the wren
the wing and the vessel of its flight
the lyre in its runic throat
the wren and the body of the wren.

The shark and the body of the shark
the sudden mouth and fix of knife
the panic shackled to the fin
the shark and the body of the shark.

The snake and the body of the snake
the twist of choking in the grass
the feet of scorpion on the tongue
the snake and the body of the snake.

The bat and the body of the bat
the flash of demi-bird and slap
the divination of the chin
the bat and the body of the bat.

EIGHT PASTORAL POEMS

(FOR JUNE & BINK NOLL)

I

It is no synod of termagants
that brings the fear of devils
to my body. The wolves of Judea
seething with speculation
hold processions on the hills.
The world's ovens make a skillet
of my bed.
An hegemony
of trumpet in the night—
like wheat in the fields of spring—
breaks through the frost
to the burning world.

II

He sings his sonnets to a witless whore
and sets no traps for hawks but weeps
and dreams of children. I've taught him
no divided love, no severance;
he was made with sweetest hassle
on my wedding day. But love's law
knows no diligence and there is rapacity
in the thoughts of sons though I hold
him dearer for his hazards. My hip sang
at his joining but sons are prodigal
and in their loves assassinate their loves.

III

Bring it down, the whole confusion
with no jot withheld, no delusion
struck from the fancy; the pindaric
mastery of praise, the feats of magnificence,
the Hun in the rubble of mallets,
iliads and panegyrics, ruckus
and vast Asian thoughts; Man, sunning
like Midas in his own chicanery.

Agamemnon as Arcady
IV

In forms of dark, in single attack,
the pheasants rose into the trees
at five. I think they sprang
from caverns in the earth
so suddenly they appeared,
so fast their rising up.

The sounds of doom are various.
With a sound that pine boughs make
when loosed from snow they spring back
into symmetry the pheasants toppled
from their trees, as if my bell
was a fowler's horn, and fell to Dis
through windows at my feet.

I thought of kites and cannibals,
and Agamemnon in his armored barge.

v

In fields of lemon trees
I dreamed of Agamemnon,
of tombs, of low pitched horns.
Bees were nuncios to the Trojan
dawn where Assassination sniffed the air
computing sweetness with its canine snout.

Black Angus sunned like caliphs
on the grass; ducks kicked
hex on the dazzling stream.

It's dynasties that shift the time
and I remembered Agamemnon stuttering
toward regalia.

VI

Depending on the angle of the sun,
a black bull or a garden beetle
sends fire down my thin body. I
have made acquaintance with Buck the Bull,
Black Minotaur, Unnatural Lamb, Assassin.

I call him Agamemnon, Buck Agamemnon,
the Bull of the Argolid, Cassandra's Animal;
Both Torero and Beast, the Beautiful Mycenian
with tendencies toward annihilation.

de Anima

VII

There is no skill like snow on a long field.
In my mind's eye I meet desolation there,
struck by the soul, extant and specified
as real as snow and panslavic as all the armies of the Turks.

Trees at the boundary of two fields are nothing
like any reckoning of man, upright there
in the sprung light; cornflowers at the threshold,
an idea of horns.
                    All things are even and odd,
all parallel, all disinterested but trees
in a long field rive the mind with color.

There was nothing in Grafton to make me wild
and twelfth night just passed had left
the blood in me cold. It was the white
of the lovely field, the two trees (bluebells
or white deer) that made me think of soul,
specified, extant, panslavic as all the armies of the Turks.

VIII

The sound of the soul
is not the sound of a bell.
It is a still clock,
a horn not touched,
a giraffe,
an idea of mallets,
being all things that would be written down
by a non-believer.

I think it is more likely to be
a hoot owl
a hoot owl and a nightingale together,
a line of drummers,
a tug-o-war,
an idea of arrows
being all things that would be written down
by a believer
                    but
I tend to think that perhaps the things of men,
believers or not, contain contradictions.

AN ART OF POETRY

I

The advantage of the line is direction
to the generate point
where torrid with gesture
it swerves upon itself
and builds the primitive arc,
deranged center, wrought circle.
For Euclid and an Arabian child
shape is not gainsaid
nor left pillared to a gathering of
inch, but must in its mode, category,
in the spring of its architecture
move fast to hoop.

II

When rhetoric begins poetry does.
In the disputation of the will
the voyages took by the eye.
In its handlings of horns
the ear will utter a lesson:
the singing of seas,
growling gulls.
When the corn in gold turrets
burns in the sun's punctual fire.
The scuffle of the scorpion
across the winter web.

Poetry begins where rhetoric does.
When poetry speaks
a theater lamentation, when it seems
Lear did mightily by the hurricane.

III

I've told you again and again
how the world began.
                            How the
elephant grew, that fish learned
the sea was best, why apes walked,
How calamity befell Eve.
How Jehovah watched like a club-footed
girl stalking a swan.
                            I've told you
that the middle-of-words are fixed
to a kite and are reachless;
though alternate and charged
the poles are still, that color
melted in flame yields nothing.

With a slow voice I've told you
love betters love, that alphabet
is Adam trying his ribs for woman.

I've told you the history of my history,
the wild Arabia of my brow, your map
to reconnoiter as you will, teeming
with the uncalamity of your boyhood.

YEATS

He played too long on passion's calliope,
this prince who walked on blood-gold sands,
who ran down streets beneath the roots of trees
and captured elephants with parts of bees.

Each rock bloomed, a neoteric seed
sprung quick from mineral acres,
proper stones gyrated from their moss,
revealed some new brand, restored some change.

To make them gods, he crammed the mouths of men
with waves of subtile flame,
and walked on appian ways to open barns
where new grain shook its birth from barrel staves.

O yeats, come my jo john,
fin of mackerel, wing of swan,
bound in braille, broken by the blind,
straight winters-men, come down,
into dublin town come down come down.

TWO HOMILIES

(FOR MARK VAN DOREN)

I

Expect this,
that rock may be supposéd bear
or any elephant may shiver
from a rose
and some undoubted seer
may hold the brainless edge of thought.
O anything may be a circle
or any man, however hump
may move like cleanest prince
through ordinary halls and
touch each foot on hunted gold.
That dark imago of a bird
may be a nun who rises
to some accident of trumpet
that merely is
a falling red balloon.
O beautiful collision
where mind meets the shaping light
and waits in adoration
while all things clang.

II

It may or may not be decisive
whether or not the sun is fire
or the lark a goddess
or the current angel incisive prodigal
or the dead mime a hyacinth
or policemen the enemy's bad dream.
This is all that will ever count;
that the sun be enough of roundness
that the rock describe the ground
that the priest carry his body high
that the river flow with the swan
that the night bring hawk and star
that some man touch with gentleness his son.

AN INCIDENT EARLY IN THE WORLD'S HISTORY

Nothing is so desperate as a favorite child.
His mother saw a prince in him: Cain,
Prince of Men, blue-eyed, head like a sunflower,
high-stepping, booted, trim as a row of oats,
fierce of arm, Eve's boy.

But there was brotherhood
to reckon with and brothers are not simply
double sons, but are apt to be disorganized
and easy to dismay. These two were a trouble
from the start—in the field, one turning
the plow by a rose, the other learning
the disposition of his flock, both watching
the sun. And then there was the twist
of the earth at the fall of rain.

The world
had just begun to set its course; the sun rose
daily in a certain place, the hills were
not fluid, nor rocks shivered in the heat:
what was land yesterday was land today,
no more sea lurching to displace the fence
and rust the plow; acres held their bounds
and onions grew deep in the straight furrow.
It was the day of the earth's settling,
of the months of thyme and sheltering trees.

But there was brotherhood to reckon with
and gods to love, and loving gods is often
out of sorts with things and apt to throw the
best of men into a fit. It was a matter
with these boys of the lamb and the vegetable,
which was best, which went up in flame hottest,
what smoke was blacker. It was a choice
of attitude and luck: Abel with his lamb,
Cain and his onion and what was nearer
to the mind of God.

And Cain lost.
In the gamble for sacrifice Cain lost and
Abel won; but winning in that family was a curse
and Abel's head got broke apart like that.
All this in the world's newness. Nothing came
before or after it so terrible and Eve and Adam,
used to falling out of grace, leaned from
their tree and pulled the ladder up.
                                    Rocks
moved in Cain's acre and in a furrow trim
as a row of oats, Abel's heart lay wound in thyme.

MYTH

I knew a man with a terrible obsession
who thought that he was fire
who would tramp the fields in hob-nail boots
turning all the timothy into ash
and all the wild geese into funerary jugs.
He had no fit so terrible as one I saw
at high noon when he turned a page
of Jeremiah and scorched the sands of Gideon
to glass. He was terrible another time
and cypresses curled like shavings at his touch;
roots yielded up their syrups and the sun
rocked in the oven of his eye. He moved
through the world, burning rivers from their beds,
tottering the centers of hoops, galvanizing
snowmen into juggernauts, and pulled up to boiling
the streams of spring. O terrible this booted colossus
this hooting flame who saw all the world
in his obsession and made it do for tinder, flint
and furnace. Hulking in the sun, rattling
among poppies he contended for dominion
in the flaring orbit of his terrible obsession.

HERO

Without the slightest strain
he slew the crude marauder
who standing near a flaming bridge
whelped his braggadocio cry
and was delivered up. Ho!

Unlimited now, he was bruited to
the northerly way. He muddled
nothing, got trapped by no
(however beautiful) lady, in no
(however splendid) garden.
Every, any, thing waked to him;
he was morning, they sleeping flowers.

The tender gorgons, double-headed imps,
rolled hoops, tossed balls into the air,
banked the toothéd wall with tulips,
soared into the trees for a go at tag
with the ape. He came to no patina
in the dirt and held fearlessly
his wand in the face of Dis, hurried
by ten shimmering girls. Lust
did not move in any natural thing.

Simply no fear in him, no meditated
ugliness. Finding avenger dull,
knight barren, seer uncomfortable,
he returned to his place, deep in a grove,
where sang, full breasted, comely birds.

L'ANNUNCIAZIONE
from Bellini

An angel stepping through her window said:
I come to you, a sign from him who sent me.
And leaving then her unbelief she told
the incident from off the sill
and bade it sit before her on the floor.

There was nothing like the fear she felt;
to have a winged and sudden thing
appear to her with not a trumpet or
a trace of wind. She bade him come and say,
if anything would say it well, the news.

He said: I bring you barns and donkeys,
satraps and camel humps, one dozen sheep,
their shepherds and their smell, a star,
a raging king, his sharp knife and a man
who cuts out windows, doors and chairs.

She said: I am used to walking and no grand
folderol of yours will still the flying wind
nor feign trumpets out of silence; connive away,
there's breach enough in any God
to answer you. I have no truck with incidents.

He said: I bring you meadow and winter,
cypress and river, white oxen in the sun,
a boy whose eyes scare dolphins high
as kites; the beautiful mirror of the incessant
zero; I bring you contradiction.

She said: I'll leave you now, you incident,
and from my sight you'll fly, leaving
your wing's shadow caught on that shutter,
your spine breaking the light. I must get
off the dream and back to filling jars.

He said: I bring you flaring squares, circles,
perpendiculars, and trapezoids; I bring you
color from the sun. I bring you
folderol. You'll be Jehovah's honeycomb.
I bring you caravans, a burglary.

She said: I will behave as filling jars were
all my life; I will decide to have a walk,
and incident, I shall not dance again
nor tremble when some doubtful thing steps on my sill.
And fell from heaven then a dominion in her womb.

A POEM ABOUT ODYSSEUS

Odysseus can be seen without all that war.
Counting out the fuss about the grand slay,
victory is not really heroic and Odysseus'
victory was just a sham; through it
other things are evident: the seashore,
the morse code fiber in the groin
sounding all the way from sandal to helmet;
sparrows on the Trojan wall
beating their wings to be burned, delaying
the southward march until they could go with blazing crests.

Homer made his way in Odysseus with gentle images,
pointing to the book, the staff, the sheep, her bed,
letting the deaths of boys look like poplar trees
undeveloped and careless in the end. . . .

The only thing that moves in the whole storybook
of Eyeless is the cape of his bright-spoken,
hot, limping, daisy-sworded, lyre-waisted,
violent, seadeepblue, unaphrodisiac, caterwauling,
cradle-legged, death-bedraggled, life-green
littlebabysoldier, Giant, who struck everything
he passed into a village crowd to burn forever
in the copper pane of his shield.

MICHELANGELO'S SCAFFOLDING

(FOR VALBORG ANDERSON)

All propped up to God
he lies awash with sinew
moving the ceiling like a bear
a rock moves
to spill the sweet and syrup
of the world out.

Debunked by wisdom
to this indolence he growls
to lift his arms to growl form
from the sleeping joint
and rout the trumpet in the vein
from hankering to attack.

The doltish gibbering back
arched to get the dream
in the Sibyl's eye, faults
it with bandito hand
and groans to bring
the groin with umber still.

This car is equipage
to him who found decrees of christus
in the corded spine
and prestidigitations of the beast
acoil in the wrist
where Adam lay.

The scaffold like a carrying
hand held him there to think
the work complete;
that nothing lack the shock
that no sweet vantage prowling the body
went unnoticed down.

MICHELANGELO
Three Lyrics in Explanation   (FOR ANNE MARIE STOKES)

I

He spoke straight to marble. Said:
"Break," and from that chisel David
fell, terrible among shepherds,
feared at games, mocker who had
brought from genesis calamity
for giants.
              And Goliath
bounded through the valley of Elah
counting judges on his fingers
strewing heads like snow in the wind
contemplating all the world
forage for his swallowing.

And legs fell and held the plain
(like filaments) teeming with Goliath
in the morning (O tendons be brave)
for a boy who'd pulled lambs
from the maws of bears had cornered
all the world like Cain
with thoughts of slaughter.

Terribilita stepped from the scaffold
and took a view of the victim
(bounding in Elah):
lariats whipped in the hammer
when he paused to scan the killing.

II *The Night of the Hammer*

Thinking on a work
changes it somehow.

Thinking of his eyes
damages my sleep.
He who cannot sleep
must bear the light.

To get, to fix, to see
the form: hard to do.

I gauged him wrong.
Marble for one leg.
(O Christ of the one leg)
A poem had found me silly

at Carrara. Thinking sonnets
turns the head from quarries.

Thinking on a work
changes it somehow.

Two laws the hammer teaches:
To destroy is to create;
To create is to destroy.
Break up the thing.

(The wheel tends to zigzag
when circles bind up Euclid's hands.)

And he took a hammer then
and smashed the God
he turned. Erupted up the
thing, thinking:

Thinking on a work
changes it somehow.

III *At Carrara*

The lay of the land struts
through this hill. I cover
my eyes; tend all scrutiny
to the void where anatomies
collapsed and metamorphosed
wrangle in the sun. I tease
the dumb geologist to find
the corpus in that gully
in this hill. I
bring forth the mud and slag
of the world and burn it to
cipher in my fist. There
is nothing to lose. The work
is done; days have come to
term and here where seed
has turned to precipice and
lizards lisp through the brush
I cleave the dark essentia
in the earth and touch
angelicum, hooded in the grain.

UCCELLO

O Uccello, Uccello
you are a cosmic
comic fellow.

I want, he said
to conceive
a
hurricane . . .

I want the
enormous wave
in my wrist.

I want
slaughter of gulls
at my throat.

I want
the lugubrious worm.

I'd see anchors pinwheels:
denizens drum fathoms.

I want, said Uccello
to conceive
the hurricane:

The brine and the fish
the dilate weed
the spindrift
the cataleptic sun
the distracted sailor
the splay-backed ray
the whale's hump . . .

(Knew too
how it felt to have
the tide rush in
up the arm
to drill the mind
in a parable of winds.)

ON SAINT THERESA'S DIFFICULTY
IN KEEPING HER FEET ON THE GROUND

She would not leap for joy
and told her nuns employ
what means they must
to keep her close to dust.

But God would not obey
and when she went to pray
he picked her up
hood, bib and all and cut

the cloister up with levitation.
She stationed nuns, gravitation
guards she called them,
a wimpled group of ten

to guard her when she knelt.
They waited; at a nod (she felt
her heels kick up) they bound
her with a length of hemp, sound

to a boulder in the wall
and held her tight. But all
for nothing; loose or trussed
they could not keep the just

from rising to the ceiling.
They had a spanish feeling
that perhaps they guarded evil
in that cell. Who pulled? Keel

over once and diabolus perhaps
would roll his eyes; slaps
and knocks of imps; a screech
of angels filled out her peach

with boils; but when she prayed
she felt balloons and strayed
into the light. She roared
and from a line of pillars poured

the guardian ten and pulled
her back to earth. Hauled
down they slid her to a chair
and staked her there

with chains into the floor.
But settled down she was tore
up again and took
on high as fishers hook

a drowsing trout out of his den.
She fought the catch; when
Christus pulled her up she let
her shoulders drop; set

her teeth on edge and fell
at the knees. If it were hell
then hell it was; but she knew
that only God would argue

on the bias; leaving tit for tat
and standing up to all that
leverage, she told the carpenters
to pry her up and loose her center's

howling gravity. No more riot
balked her rising up. In the quiet
of halls of nunnery they saw
their mother floating grandly through the door.

How did it happen that Noni, the boy, and his dog, Nimuk, were on a floating iceberg with nothing to eat?

(from a grammar-school reader)

Because Noni trespassed in the night
near the window of Nimuk's woman;
Because the seed in the arctic
grows cold in Noni's thigh
and broke to lustiness
and set the heart
adrift . . .

Because
in mind
nothing is left to feed upon
when the blood is cold;
the hands fixed with ice to the jaw;
Because Noni went where
Nimuk slept God broke apart and
thumped . . .

Because the grass of the north is blue
with wind, Noni
came to Nimuk in the night when
the snow burned and the bear
took advantage of the dark;
terrible doings, done:
done with swift but
patient teeth . . .

Because
floating on
an iceberg with nothing
to eat but each other; no sauce;
but in the brain the bowl's image and
the overflowing flex of bread and meat, real
in both this dog and man: intellect's scan of gullet . . .

Because of this, Nimuk
came to Noni in the night; prayer, bed,
post of cedar, could not allay the
awful supper in his maw; and
Noni died, alone, torn and
head down, in pillow.

TO A MONK WHO FOUND
HE COULD NOT WRITE POETRY
AFTER HE HAD RECOVERED
FROM A LONG ILLNESS *(Downside Abbey, 1956)*

Dulcis and then all misericordia gone
and your body fell into place again.
Undone by pain, the shock received
and reckoned with, the blood, long after
ruckus, divulged its light and brought you
to your feet in a sweet salience of nerves.
But you lost all your hunger for
two rhymed words and leaned no more
toward the far off verb; genius
sought out the unordained who shivered
in the mother house with rubrics
uncontested in his brain. That's the way
it is: when you're used to sleep
the night goes: when the beloved's back
curves into the grass an owl horned
and void hoots the grove to bits:
when winds roar the memories of floods
return and the wind bears up the law
from the sea. When the bee in the bonnet
turns everything to poetry and the world,
a tumult of syllables, knocks
like an engine in the fingertips, it is time
for the long and terrible caterwauling
that seals the humors and makes all physicians dumb.

THE SAVAGE

(FOR MICHAEL SCOTT)

The roar of birth falls down you
like morning in the air.
The ocean, pen of fish and shell
plays to rush about your heart.
A craven and recording self
blows his laughter in your face.
You hear the matters that destroy,
the sweet idea grammarian,
that love is gypsum to the flame
that comes to shape your bountied head.

You seem to be a single thing,
a garden circumscribed within,
or color from a pirate's cap.
The tiger and the parrot watch,
and see their fanfare in your eyes.

Like a stone falling in the ocean's
deepest place, the shock of beauty
forever favors you and draws you out
in reaches full of light.

And hot contends with hot
and the ape expels its soul in forestry
as Savage brings the whole world down
in stratagems of eye and head.

ON TURNING THE PAGE OF A JEWELED BOOK

(FOR DOROTHY HAM CORBIN)

I turned the page of a jeweled book
and read the singing of a word
held in notes black as spinsters' jade.
On a plain of gold, raised up with bars
of stem, a silver vine spelled "A"
and ran therefrom a runway pressed with
pearl where double "L" speared with
rubies and delphic leaf grew in a maze
of swan. "E" guyed to a griffin
with ropes of ash flared to an almond
tree where angels' bodies filled the page
down to Amen and harassed "L" amid
their wings. "U" was white on white
(like Mondrian but whiter)
and from the lift of the swerves'
crest two fleur-de-lys sprang up
erect as clarinets. In a thicket
three hounds barked a ferret from
his den where "I" complained like a sybil
from the depth. In a rain of runic heads
the final "A" lay cased about with wind.
And when I let the page fall back
(for I went on to search beginnings out)
I heard a sound of horns as when a
quarry tracked to death is stranded in an oak.

THE COMPLAINT OF A YOUNG PRIEST
(FOR CHARLES MAC ISSAC)

I hear the golden lion rage,
                    the phoenix
crash in fire where it wished to go.
Krishna on a spinning stick
               a vision
breaks from the greenwood tree,
an egyptian head turns upward,
                  someone
leaves the holocaust and returns to love;
a momentary unicorn passes by the sun,
a flood of robins suffer a partial song
                   and
sheltered by this low fence I lean like
a widow from her porch when a girl in the garden
crushes her youth's body in the night
filling the ground with pain.
                I cannot
stay within this house; the doorsill
heaves, reason and its geometry
disturb the saints upon the wall
and I recall the deaf child
who wept at the death of birds.
               When
the sun comes up behind the Lady of the Seven Sorrows
I hear the music of the hoodlum in the night.
I see the flower in his hat.
             The angel
roars in the pleasure of its own fantasy.

Sacrifice is the thing I do.
I am anointed to incur the heat
and not burn; faced with gold, feel the lacquer
and know the hive where there is hurricane
and honey the bee cannot make.

There is other knowledge than the words
the lack of woman makes. What my hands touch
and cannot feel, what my throat tastes and cannot
taste. The absence of the sensual
where the sensuous is all whir and hum.
                                        Twice before
I have complained to the center of the sun; when
I was forced into the sea to find a golden ring
and when my hand had traced itself with slaughter.

Now the third time and the endlessness of it.
Without tune, without alphabet, touched by the
                                        certainty

that destroys, I find the white dove
sulking in the tabernacle.

ADJECTIVES TOWARD THE DESCRIPTION OF A CRUCIFIX

(FOR RICHARD FREMANTLE)

I

Cruciform to begin with, the plain word,
telling the direction of the wood, how
the fabricator's hands took up the task
and why instead of that way he turned it
this.

II

Inhabited perhaps would say it well:
that the cross-bow slung in the bowl
held a vacancy for dying.

III

Combustible, to make it clear it held
a greek-fire like a tool and had in its
heyday the seeds of expiration tearing
through it.

IV

A canzone because these songs are crisscrossed
with rhyme which catches up the tags of sense.
Crucifixion was all that and caught up
the logos, husk and all.

V

A belltower in a full and flowering field
where bees announce the release of cannon
and the hive goes dead with exodus.
(A word at least to denote that
the pulling of ropes can suffocate with ritual.)

VI

Two children since they often hang up
life on the breadth of two bent sticks
and whip the viper out of hollyhocks.

VII

Wasp would do for an animal: when a wasp
gets tripped up in a lizard's jaw
and needles crackle outside time.

VIII

A hammock to say clearly that after
the sun had sprinted through him
and fetched him tired to a shade
foresters picked his tree and would not let go.

IX

A barge in a countersea: the final word.
Beached.
Hasped and fired.
Builded.

THIS WILL BE THE SONG

I

This will be the song and the sound of it:
the light of a yellow bird in the sun,
the light of day burning in a tree
when green turns gold with growing:
a bright body forcing the clenched eye
open; song will be hid in a boy who
walks the ocean where the mammoth turtle
creeps. These words will break the
hieroglyphic waters of the sea
where zero shuts the wind in ice
and heaves the wind in a captivity.
Nothing is bright like fields of wheat,
nothing various like a hill of flowers
moving like rivers in the light.

II

This will be the song and the sound of it:
the dark water of the darkest ocean,
the dark trees of the forest where
Behemoth stalks; the dark body of a lady
whose hair is terrible. Song will be
hid in the interior of a stone
and the word will be dark in a
possessed and chromatic alphabet. Song
will be sung by the darkest child
in the most terrible summer day
when the sunflower turns the sunlight out,
as youth in the night hears body shout.
My hand is dark and darkness is sound
and my song in darkness will be found.